Start And Grow Rich

The Ultimate Guide To Small Business Success
Jules Beshears

Copyright © 2023 by Jules Beshears / 414 Industries

All rights reserved.

No portion of this book may be reproduced in any form without written permission from the publisher or author, except as permitted by U.S. copyright law.

Contents

....1
1. Introduction 2
2. Understanding Your Target Market 3
3. Conducting Market Research 5
4. Writing a Business Plan...8
5. Securing Funding for Your Small Business 11
6. Choosing the Right Business Structure 14
7. Building Your Brand 17
8. Marketing Strategies for Small Businesses 20
9. Managing Finances and Accounting 23
10. Operating and Growing Your Small Business 26
11. Legal Considerations for Small Business Owners 29
12. Navigating Challenges and Risks................................32
13. Staying Competitive in the Market.............................35
14. Strategies for Success and Expansion 38
15. Conclusion and Next Steps for Your Small Business Venture ..41

1.
2.
3.
4.
5.
6.
7.
8.
9.
10.
11.
12.
13.
14.

15.

This book is dedicated to my family, friends, and entrepreneurs who refused to give up. To those entrepreneurs like myself for whom failure was not an option.

Chapter 1

Introduction

Starting a small business can be a challenging but rewarding experience. It provides the opportunity to be your own boss, work on something you're passionate about, and make a difference in the lives of others. However, coming up with a business idea can be daunting, especially when there is so much competition. This chapter aims to provide you with an overview of small business ideas and help you get started on the path to entrepreneurship.

Small businesses come in all shapes and sizes, and there is no one-size-fits-all approach. Some small businesses are based on a specific skill or talent, while others focus on solving a particular problem. Some cater to a specific niche or target market, and others offer a unique product or service.

The key to success is finding an idea that aligns with your interests, skills, and values. You want to choose something you enjoy doing, know about, and can provide a sustainable income. This way, you will be motivated to put in the hard work and effort required to build and grow your business.

We will explore various small business ideas, including online businesses, service-based businesses, product-based businesses, and franchising. We will also discuss the importance of understanding your target market, conducting market research, and writing a business plan. By the end of this chapter, you will have a better understanding of what it takes to start a small business and be inspired to pursue your entrepreneurial dreams.

Chapter 2

Understanding Your Target Market

One of the essential steps in starting a small business is understanding your target market. Your target market refers to the group of people whom you are aiming to sell your products or services. Understanding your target market is crucial because it helps you tailor your marketing efforts, design your products or services, and price them effectively.

To understand your target market, you need to start by conducting market research. Market research involves gathering information about your potential customers, including their demographics, needs, and preferences. This information can be obtained through various methods, including surveys, focus groups, and secondary research.

Once you have conducted market research, you can use the information to create a buyer persona. A buyer persona is a fictional representation of your ideal customer based on the data you have collected. It includes their age, income, education level, and buying habits. A clear understanding of your buyer persona can help you make informed decisions about your marketing, product development, and sales strategies.

Another critical aspect of understanding your target market is identifying their needs and pain points. This involves understanding the problems or challenges that your target customers face and how your products or services can help solve them. By addressing the needs of your target market, you are more likely to attract and retain customers and build a strong brand.

It is important to note that your target market may change over time, and it is essential to continually review and update your market research. Keeping up-to-date with changes in your target market can help you stay competitive and grow your business.

Understanding your target market also helps you communicate effectively with your customers. Knowing their preferences allows you to tailor your messaging and marketing efforts to resonate with them. This can lead to increased engagement, brand loyalty, and customer satisfaction.

Moreover, having a deep understanding of your target market can help you make informed decisions about your product or service offerings. You can develop products and services that specifically cater to the needs of your target customers, which can give you a competitive advantage in the market.

It is also important to remember that your target market is not limited to your current customers. You can identify new opportunities and expand your target market by continuously conducting market research. This can help you grow your business and increase your revenue.

In short, understanding your target market is crucial for the success of your small business. It helps you make informed decisions, communicate effectively with customers, and stay competitive in the market. So, invest time and effort into understanding your target market, and you will be well on your way to success.

Chapter 3

Conducting Market Research

Market research is critical in starting a small business, as it provides valuable information about your target market and helps inform your business decisions. Market research involves gathering data and information about your industry, target market, and competitors, which can be used to make informed decisions about your business strategy.

There are various market research methods, including primary and secondary research. Primary research involves collecting data directly from your target market through surveys, focus groups, and customer interviews. Secondary research involves using existing data and resources, such as market reports, industry publications, and government statistics.

When conducting market research, it is essential to focus on the following key areas:

1. **Industry trends:** Understanding your industry's current and future trends can help you make informed decisions about your business strategy.
2. **Target market:** Gather information about your target market, including their demographics, needs, and buying habits. This information can be used to create a buyer persona.
3. **Competitors:** Analyze the strengths and weaknesses of your competitors and determine how you can differentiate yourself in the market.

4. **Customer needs:** Identify your target customers' needs and pain points and determine how your products or services can help solve them.
5. **Market size:** Estimate the size of your target market and determine if there is enough demand for your products or services.

Using multiple sources of information and data to validate your market research findings is important. This will ensure that your conclusions are accurate and reliable and that you comprehensively understand your market.

Additionally, it is important to remember that market research should not be a one-time event. It is essential to continually monitor and update your research to stay informed about changes in your industry and target market. This will help you make informed decisions about your business strategy and respond to changes in the market in a timely manner.

Moreover, market research can also help you identify new opportunities and trends in your industry. This can help you stay ahead of your competitors and capture new markets.

When conducting market research, it is vital to be objective and impartial. Avoid biases and personal opinions, and focus on gathering and analyzing data to make informed decisions.

Lastly, it is crucial to consider the cost and time involved in conducting market research. Various low-cost or free resources are available for market research, including online surveys and government statistics. Consider your budget and resources when planning your market research, and prioritize the most important information for your business.

In conclusion, conducting market research is an ongoing process that can provide valuable information to inform your business decisions and help you stay competitive. So, make market research a priority in your business planning, and you will be well on your way to success.

Chapter 4

Writing a Business Plan

A business plan is a critical document for starting a small business, as it outlines your business strategy and provides a roadmap for success. A well-written business plan can also help you secure funding from investors or lending institutions, as it demonstrates your understanding of the market and the potential for your business.

When writing a business plan, it is important to include the following key elements:

1. **Executive Summary:** This is a brief overview of your business, including your mission, products or services, target market, and financial projections.
2. **Company Description:** Describe your business, including its history, structure, and management team.
3. **Market Analysis:** Provide an in-depth analysis of your industry, target market, and competitors, including market trends and customer needs.
4. **Product or Service Offerings:** Describe your products or services in detail, including their unique selling points and benefits.
5. **Marketing and Sales Strategy:** Outline your plans for marketing and selling your products or services, including your target market, marketing channels, and sales tactics.

6. **Financial Projections:** Provide financial projections for your business, including sales projections, expenses, and profitability.
7. **Funding Requirements:** Outline your funding requirements, including the funding you seek and how you plan to use the funds.

When writing a business plan, it is essential to be detailed and realistic. Use clear and concise language, and provide supporting data and research to validate your assumptions and projections.

Additionally, it is crucial to continually update your business plan as your business grows and evolves. Regularly reviewing and updating your business plan can help ensure that you are on track to meet your goals and stay competitive in the market.

It is also essential to seek the help of experts when writing your business plan, especially if you are unfamiliar with financial projections or legal requirements. You can consult a business coach, accountant, or attorney to help create a professional and accurate business plan.

Another valuable tool for writing a business plan is to use templates and examples from successful businesses. You can find many templates and examples online or from your local Small Business Administration (SBA) office. These can help guide you in the right direction and give you a better understanding of what should be included in your business plan.

In addition, it is important to consider your audience when writing a business plan. If you are seeking funding from investors or lending institutions, it is vital to present a clear and professional business plan that demonstrates your understanding of the market and the potential for your business. On the other hand, if you are writing a business plan for internal use, you can be more flexible and creative in your approach.

Finally, be prepared to make changes and revisions to your business plan as you receive feedback and new information. A business plan is not a static document and should be updated regularly to reflect changes in your business and the market.

In conclusion, writing a business plan requires time and effort, but it is a critical step in starting a small business. By seeking help from experts, using templates and examples, and being prepared to make changes, you can create a professional and accurate business plan that will help you achieve your goals and succeed in the market.

Chapter 5

Securing Funding for Your Small Business

Securing funding is critical in starting a small business, as it can provide the necessary capital to start and grow your business. Various funding options are available, including personal savings, loans from lending institutions, and investments from angel investors or venture capitalists.

When seeking funding for your small business, it is crucial to consider the following factors:

1. **Business Plan:** A well-written business plan is critical to securing funding, as it demonstrates your understanding of the market and the potential for your business.
2. **Credit History:** Your personal and business credit history can impact your ability to secure funding, so it is vital to review your credit reports and take steps to improve your credit score if necessary.
3. **Collateral:** Some funding options may require collateral, such as real estate or equipment, to secure the loan. Consider the assets you have available to use as collateral and the potential impact on your business.
4. **Cost of Capital:** Consider the cost of capital, including interest rates, fees, and repayment terms, when evaluating funding options. Choose the option that best aligns with your business goals and financial projections.

5. **Investor Network:** Building relationships with angel investors or venture capitalists can provide opportunities for investment in your business. Consider attending networking events, participating in pitch competitions, and seeking referrals from trusted sources.

When seeking funding for your small business, it is vital to be prepared and professional. Research the funding options available, understand the requirements and criteria for each option and be ready to provide a clear and compelling pitch to potential investors or lenders.

Additionally, consider seeking the help of a business coach, accountant, or attorney to help you navigate the funding process and secure the best deal for your business.

It is also essential to have a clear understanding of how much funding you need and how you will use the funds. A detailed financial plan and budget can help you determine the amount of funding required and provide a roadmap for how you will use the funds to grow your business.

Another important factor to consider is the type of funding that best suits your needs. For example, a loan may provide the capital you need but requires regular repayments. In contrast, an investor may provide more flexible financing but requires giving up a portion of ownership in your business.

It is also essential to be aware of the risks involved in securing funding. For example, taking on too much debt can put your business in a difficult financial position, while giving up too much equity can limit your control over your business.

In addition, be prepared to negotiate the terms of your funding, including interest rates, repayment terms, and ownership stakes. Having a clear understanding of your business plan, financial projections, and market potential can help you negotiate favorable terms that align with your goals and minimize the risks for your business.

Securing funding for your small business requires careful consideration of the funding options available, the necessary amount of funding, and the risks involved. By being prepared, professional, and knowledgeable, you can secure the funding you need to start and grow your successful business.

Chapter 6

Choosing the Right Business Structure

Choosing the Right Business Structure

Choosing the proper business structure is an important decision for any small business owner, as it can have a significant impact on taxes, liability, and management. There are several business structures to choose from, including sole proprietorship, partnership, limited liability company (LLC), corporation, and cooperative.

When choosing the proper business structure, it is important to consider the following factors:

1. **Liability:** Different business structures offer different levels of protection from personal liability for business debts and lawsuits. For example, a corporation provides limited liability for its owners, while a sole proprietorship does not.
2. **Taxes:** Different business structures also have different tax implications. For example, a corporation is taxed as a separate entity, while a sole proprietorship is taxed as personal income.
3. **Management:** The structure of your business can also impact how it is managed. For example, a corporation has a board of directors and shareholders, while the owner governs a sole proprietorship.
4. **Capital:** Consider your business's capital requirements and your business structure's ability to raise funds. For example, a corporation may have more options for raising capital than a sole proprietorship.

5. **Legal Requirements:** Each business structure has different legal requirements, such as registering with the state, filing annual reports, and maintaining corporate records.

It is important to consider the advantages and disadvantages of each business structure and seek the advice of a business coach, accountant, or attorney to help you choose the right structure for your business.

Additionally, it is important to understand that you can change your business structure as your business grows and evolves. For example, you may start as a sole proprietorship and later switch to an LLC or corporation as your business expands. It is essential to regularly review your business structure and make changes as necessary to ensure that it continues to meet your needs and support the growth of your business.

Furthermore, it is also essential to stay informed of the legal and tax requirements associated with your chosen business structure. For example, you may be required to file annual reports, pay business taxes, and maintain certain records. Failing to comply with these requirements can result in fines and legal penalties, so it is vital to understand and adhere to the obligations associated with your business structure.

Finally, it is important to have a comprehensive understanding of the implications of your business structure on your business operations, such as decision-making, ownership, and control. This understanding will help you ensure that your structure supports the goals and vision of your business and enables you to make informed decisions that promote its success.

In summary, choosing the proper business structure is an ongoing process that requires careful consideration, regular review, and a comprehensive understanding of its implications for your business. By following these guidelines, you can make informed decisions that support the growth and success of your small business.

Chapter 7

Building Your Brand

Building a strong brand is essential for any small business, as it helps to differentiate your business from competitors and create a lasting impression with customers. A well-defined brand also helps to establish credibility and trust with customers, which is essential for building and maintaining long-term relationships.

The following are key elements to consider when building your brand:

1. **Mission and Values:** Define the mission and values of your business and make sure that your brand reflects these values and aligns with your business goals.
2. **Target Market:** Identify your target market and understand their needs and preferences. This information can help you to tailor your branding to appeal to your target market and build a strong connection with them.
3. **Name and Logo:** Choose a memorable and unique name and logo that represents your brand and appeals to your target market. Your name and logo should be easily recognizable and consistent across all marketing materials.
4. **Brand Voice:** Develop a consistent brand voice that reflects your mission, values, and target market. This can include elements such as tone, language, and messaging and should be used consistently across your marketing materials.

5. **Visual Identity:** Create a visual identity for your brand, including elements such as color palette, typography, and imagery. This visual identity should be consistent across all of your marketing materials and help to reinforce your brand identity.
6. **Marketing Strategy:** Develop a comprehensive marketing strategy that includes advertising, public relations, content marketing, and social media. Your marketing strategy should be consistent with your brand identity and help to reinforce your brand message and values.

It's important to note that building a brand is an ongoing process that requires consistent effort and attention. This means that you should regularly review and refine your brand to ensure that it continues to reflect the changing needs and preferences of your target market and supports your business's goals and vision.

Moreover, your brand should also be integrated into every aspect of your business operations, from customer service to product development. This helps to ensure that your brand is consistent and reinforced across all touchpoints with customers and supports your business's overall success.

In order to build a strong brand, it may also be beneficial to seek outside help, such as working with a branding specialist or marketing agency. These professionals can provide valuable insights, guidance, and support as you develop and refine your brand and can help to ensure that your brand supports the growth and success of your business.

Finally, it is important to recognize that building a brand takes time, effort, and patience. However, the investment in building a solid brand can pay off in the long run, as it helps to establish a strong foundation for your business and sets the stage for future growth and success.

In summary, building a strong brand is an ongoing process that requires careful consideration, consistent effort, and a comprehensive understanding of the needs and preferences of your target market. By following these guidelines and seeking outside help as needed, you can build a brand that supports the growth and success of your small business.

Chapter 8

Marketing Strategies for Small Businesses

Marketing is a critical component of any small business, as it helps to reach and engage potential customers, build brand awareness, and drive sales and revenue. However, many small businesses have limited budgets for marketing, which makes it essential to choose strategies that are cost-effective and impactful.

The following are some effective marketing strategies for small businesses:

1. **Content Marketing:** Develop and distribute valuable and relevant content that engages your target market and helps to build trust and credibility. This can include blog posts, infographics, videos, and other content that educate and inform your target market.

2. **Social Media Marketing:** Utilize social media platforms to reach and engage your target market, build brand awareness, and drive traffic to your website. Consider using platforms such as Facebook, Instagram, and Twitter to connect with your target market and promote your business.

3. **Email Marketing:** Develop and distribute targeted email campaigns to reach your target market and promote your products or services. This can include newsletters, promotional offers, and email content that engage your target market and drive sales.

4. **Referral Marketing:** Encourage satisfied customers to refer friends and family to your business and offer referral incentives, such as discounts or special promotions.
5. **Local SEO:** Optimize your website for local search engines, such as Google My Business, to help your business appear in local search results and reach potential customers in your area.
6. **Influencer Marketing:** Partner with influencers in your industry or niche to reach and engage your target market and build brand awareness.
7. **Event Marketing:** Host or participate in events, such as trade shows or community events, to reach and engage your target market and promote your business.

Additionally, it's important to measure and track the success of your marketing efforts so that you can continuously refine and improve your strategies. Use tools such as Google Analytics, email marketing software, and social media analytics to track key metrics, such as website traffic, engagement rates, and conversion rates.

Also, consider testing different strategies and tactics to determine what works best for your business and target market. For example, you may try different types of content, different email subject lines, or different influencer partnerships and measure the impact on your target market to see what resonates and drives results.

Another key aspect of successful marketing for small businesses is to stay up-to-date with the latest trends and developments in your industry or niche. Attend conferences, read industry publications, and participate in online communities to stay informed and find new and innovative ways to reach and engage your target market.

Finally, don't be afraid to experiment and take risks with your marketing. While it's essential to have a solid plan and strategy in place, being open to trying new approaches and exploring new opportunities can help to drive innovation and success for your business.

Effective marketing strategies for small businesses require careful planning, continuous refinement, and an ongoing commitment to staying up-to-date with industry trends and best practices. By following these guidelines and measuring the impact of your marketing efforts, you can build a successful marketing program that supports the growth and success of your small business.

Chapter 9

Managing Finances and Accounting

Proper financial management and accounting are essential for the success of any small business. This includes keeping accurate records of all financial transactions, monitoring cash flow, and making informed decisions about allocating resources.

The following are some critical steps to effectively manage your finances and accounting as a small business owner:

1. **Keep Accurate Financial Records:** Maintain detailed records of all financial transactions, including income and expenses, to ensure that you have a clear understanding of the financial health of your business. This can be done using a manual ledger or accounting software such as QuickBooks or Xero.

2. **Monitor Cash Flow:** Regularly review your cash flow statement to ensure that you have enough cash on hand to cover operating expenses and to make essential investments in your business. Use cash flow projections to anticipate any potential shortfalls and plan accordingly.

3. **Set Up a Budget:** Develop a budget to help you manage your finances effectively and stay on track with your goals. Include all projected expenses, including fixed costs such as rent and utilities, as well as variable costs such as marketing and advertising.

4. **Manage Debt:** If you have debt, manage it effectively by making regular payments and paying off the debt as quickly as possible. Consider using tools such as debt consolidation or balance transfer credit cards to help you manage your debt more effectively.
5. **Stay Up-to-Date with Tax Requirements:** Stay informed about tax laws and regulations and ensure that you are paying all required taxes on time. Consider working with an accountant or tax professional to help you navigate tax requirements and minimize your tax liability.
6. **Monitor Your Profit and Loss:** Review your profit and loss (P&L) statement regularly to ensure that you are generating enough revenue to cover your expenses and make a profit. Use this information to make informed decisions about pricing, costs, and other financial matters.
7. **Seek Professional Advice:** Consider working with a financial advisor or accountant to help you manage your finances and accounting effectively. They can help you with budgeting, tax planning, and other financial management tasks and provide valuable insights and advice as you grow your business.

Additionally, it's important to regularly review and analyze your financial statements to gain a clear understanding of your business's financial performance and identify areas for improvement. This can include reviewing profit and loss statements, balance sheets, and cash flow statements.

Another important aspect of managing finances and accounting is to have systems in place to track and manage accounts payable and receivable. This includes promptly invoicing customers for work completed, following up on late payments, and paying suppliers and other bills in a timely manner to maintain positive relationships and avoid financial difficulties.

Regarding tax planning, it's crucial to stay informed about changes to tax laws and regulations and understand the tax implications of your business activities. Consider setting aside funds each month to cover expected tax obligations, and work with a tax professional to ensure that you take advantage of all available tax incentives and deductions.

Finally, it's essential to have a solid plan in place for managing and protecting your business's financial assets. This can include implementing internal controls, such as the segregation of duties, to prevent fraud and safeguard against financial mismanagement. Additionally, consider insurance coverage, such as liability insurance, to protect against potential financial losses.

In conclusion, effective management of finances and accounting requires careful planning, ongoing monitoring and analysis, and a commitment to staying informed about tax laws and regulations. By following these guidelines and seeking the advice of professionals when necessary, you can ensure the financial stability and success of your small business.

Chapter 10

Operating and Growing Your Small Business

Once you have established your small business, it's important to focus on operating and growing it effectively. The following are some key steps to help you achieve this:

1. **Maintain Strong Customer Relationships:** Maintaining strong relationships with customers is essential to the success of your business. Encourage customer feedback and strive to provide excellent customer service to build a loyal customer base.
2. **Stay Competitive:** Stay informed about changes in your industry and the marketplace, and continuously evaluate your business processes and products to ensure that you remain competitive.
3. **Diversify Your Products or Services:** Consider expanding your offerings to include new products or services that complement your existing offerings and meet the needs of your customers.
4. **Seek Out New Markets:** Consider exploring new markets, either domestically or internationally, to increase your customer base and increase sales.
5. **Invest in Your Business:** Consider investing in new technology, equipment, or training for your employees to improve your business processes and increase efficiency.

6. **Foster a Positive Workplace Culture:** Foster a positive workplace culture by valuing and empowering your employees and promoting teamwork and collaboration.
7. **Stay Adaptable:** Stay adaptable and be prepared to pivot your business strategy as necessary in response to changes in the market or customer needs.
8. **Continuously Evaluate Your Progress:** Continuously evaluate your business's performance and make changes as necessary to improve efficiency, increase sales, and achieve your goals.

Additionally, it's important to have systems in place for tracking and analyzing key performance indicators (KPIs) such as sales, customer satisfaction, and employee engagement. This information can provide valuable insights into the health of your business and inform decision-making about areas for improvement.

Networking and building partnerships with other businesses in your industry can also be a valuable way to grow your business. Look for opportunities to collaborate on projects or cross-promote each other's products or services. This can help to increase your exposure to new customers and provide a competitive advantage.

Another aspect of operating and growing your small business is managing and developing your team. Invest in your employees by providing training and development opportunities and encouraging professional growth and career advancement. This can improve employee satisfaction, increase productivity, and lead to long-term success for your business.

Finally, it's crucial to maintain a positive work-life balance, not only for yourself but also for your employees. This can include flexible scheduling, opportunities for remote work, and programs for employee wellness and stress management. By prioritizing the well-being of your employees, you can create a more positive and productive work environment and support the long-term success of your business.

Operating and growing a small business requires a combination of innovative business practices, strong relationships, and a commitment to continuous improvement. By following these guidelines and seeking the advice of professionals when necessary, you can ensure the success and growth of your small business.

Chapter 11

Legal Considerations for Small Business Owners

Starting and operating a small business involves navigating a complex legal landscape, and it's important to be aware of the various legal considerations that may impact your business. The following are some key areas to consider:

1. **Business Structure:** It's important to choose the right business structure for your business, such as a sole proprietorship, partnership, limited liability company (LLC), or corporation. Each type of business structure has its legal implications, so it's important to understand the pros and cons of each before making a decision.

2. **Intellectual Property:** If you plan to develop and sell products or services that are unique to your business, it's important to protect your intellectual property through patents, trademarks, or copyrights. This can help to prevent others from using your ideas or products without your permission.

3. **Contracts:** Contracts are a crucial component of many business transactions, and it's important to understand the legal implications of each contract you enter into. This includes reviewing the terms and conditions of contracts with suppliers, customers, employees, and contractors.

4. **Labor Laws:** Understanding labor laws is essential to operating a compliant and fair workplace. This includes laws

related to minimum wage, overtime, and worker classification, as well as laws pertaining to employment discrimination and sexual harassment.

5. **Tax Obligations:** Small business owners have a number of tax obligations, including registering for taxes, paying estimated taxes, and filing tax returns. It's essential to understand your tax obligations and comply with them to avoid penalties and fines.

6. **Insurance:** Insurance can help protect your business from various risks, including liability and property damage. Consider purchasing insurance to protect your business against potential losses.

7. **Permits and Licenses:** Many small businesses are required to obtain permits and licenses to operate legally. It's important to understand the requirements for your specific business and comply with them to avoid legal penalties and fines.

It's essential to stay informed about changes to laws and regulations that may impact your business. This can include changes to tax laws, labor laws, and regulations related to your industry. Regularly reviewing your legal and regulatory requirements can help you stay ahead of any changes and ensure that your business is always in compliance.

Another important consideration is protecting your business from legal disputes and liability. This can include having written policies and procedures in place for employees, as well as clear contracts with suppliers, customers, and partners. Proper documentation can help to minimize the risk of legal disputes and ensure that your business is protected in the event of a lawsuit.

Finally, having a strong understanding of business laws and regulations can help you make informed decisions about the future of your business. This can include decisions related to hiring employees, entering into contracts, and expanding your business. By having a clear understanding of your legal obligations and the legal landscape, you can make decisions that support the long-term success of your business.

Understanding the legal considerations for small business owners is a critical aspect of running a successful business. By seeking the advice of legal professionals and staying informed about changes to laws and regulations, you can ensure that your business is continuously operating legally and in compliance with all relevant laws and regulations.

Chapter 12

Navigating Challenges and Risks

Running a small business involves managing a variety of challenges and risks, and it's important to have a plan in place to navigate these obstacles and ensure the success of your business. The following are some key areas to consider:

1. **Competition:** Competition is a natural part of doing business, and it's important to understand your competition and the market in which you operate. This can include conducting market research to understand consumer trends and the competitive landscape, as well as keeping up-to-date on industry news and developments.

2. **Economic Downturns:** Economic downturns can have a significant impact on small businesses, and it's essential to be prepared for these challenges. Consider developing a contingency plan that includes strategies for cost-cutting and reducing expenses during tough economic times.

3. **Cash Flow Management:** Cash flow is critical to the success of any small business, and it's important to have a solid plan in place to manage your cash flow. This can include developing a budget, tracking expenses, and maintaining healthy accounts receivable and payable.

4. **Regulatory Changes:** Regulations and laws affecting small businesses can change frequently, and it's important to stay informed about these changes and how they may impact your

business. Regularly reviewing your legal and regulatory requirements can help you stay ahead of any changes and ensure that your business is always in compliance.
5. **Hiring and Managing Employees:** Hiring and managing employees is a significant challenge for many small businesses, and it's important to have a plan in place to handle these responsibilities effectively. This can include developing clear policies and procedures for employees, as well as regular training and supporting your team.
6. **Cybersecurity:** Cybersecurity is a growing concern for small businesses, and it's essential to have a plan in place to protect your business and customers' information. This can include using secure passwords, regularly updating software, and training employees on best practices for cybersecurity.
7. **Natural Disasters:** Natural disasters, such as hurricanes, earthquakes, and fires, can have a significant impact on small businesses. It's important to have a disaster recovery plan in place to ensure that your business can recover quickly and effectively in the event of a natural disaster.

Additionally, it's vital to seek out resources and support from other small business owners, professional organizations, and government agencies to help navigate the challenges and risks of running a small business. Joining local business organizations and participating in training programs can also provide valuable insights and help you stay up-to-date on the latest developments and best practices in your industry.

It's also important to regularly evaluate and reassess your business plan and risk management strategies to ensure that they are still relevant and effective. Periodically monitoring the health of your business, including financial performance and customer satisfaction, can also provide valuable insights and help you identify potential challenges and risks before they become larger problems.

Ultimately, the key to navigating challenges and risks in small business ownership is to stay informed, stay proactive, and stay resilient. With the right resources and support, you can successfully navigate the challenges and risks of running a small business and achieve long-term success.

Chapter 13

Staying Competitive in the Market

In today's fast-paced business environment, staying competitive is crucial for the success of a small business. The following are some key strategies for staying ahead of the competition:

1. **Know Your Customers:** Understanding your target market is critical to staying competitive. Regularly conducting market research and gathering customer feedback can help you identify their needs, preferences, and changing trends. This information can then be used to inform product development and marketing strategies.

2. **Offer Unique and Valuable Products or Services:** Offering unique and valuable products, or services that meet your customers' needs can help set your business apart from the competition. This can include developing innovative products, offering specialized services, or providing exceptional customer service.

3. **Stay Current with Industry Trends:** Keeping up-to-date on industry trends and developments can help you stay ahead of the competition. Regularly attending industry conferences and events, reading trade publications, and staying informed about advancements in technology can provide valuable insights and help you stay ahead of the curve.

4. **Utilize Digital Marketing:** Digital marketing has become an essential tool for reaching customers and staying competitive.

Utilizing a range of digital marketing strategies, such as search engine optimization, social media marketing, and email marketing, can help you reach new customers and increase brand awareness.

5. **Focus on Continuous Improvement:** Continuous improvement is a crucial factor in staying competitive. Regularly reviewing and refining your business processes, products, and services can help you stay ahead of the competition and meet the changing needs of your customers.
6. **Foster Strong Relationships with Suppliers and Partners:** Building strong relationships with suppliers and partners can help you stay competitive by providing access to new products, services, and technologies. Regularly communicating with your suppliers and partners and exploring new opportunities for collaboration can help you stay ahead of the competition.
7. **Develop a Strong Company Culture:** Developing a strong company culture that values innovation, customer satisfaction, and teamwork can help you attract and retain top talent and stay competitive. Providing ongoing training and development opportunities for employees can also help your business stay ahead of the curve.

Additionally, it's important to stay nimble and adaptable in order to respond to changes in the market and capitalize on new opportunities. Being open to new ideas and approaches, experimenting with new strategies, and continuously learning and evolving can help you stay competitive and stay ahead of the curve.

Another critical factor in staying competitive is understanding your competition. Regularly monitoring your competitors' activities, including their products, services, pricing, marketing strategies, and customer feedback, can provide valuable insights and help you stay ahead of the competition. This information can also be used to inform your own business strategies and make adjustments as needed.

Finally, staying competitive requires a commitment to excellence and a focus on delivering value to your customers. Providing high-quality products and services, responding promptly to customer needs and concerns, and consistently providing an exceptional customer experience can help you build customer loyalty and stay competitive in the market.

Staying competitive in the market requires a combination of staying informed, staying nimble, staying focused on customer needs, and staying committed to excellence. By continuously improving and evolving, small businesses can remain competitive, reach new customers, and achieve long-term success.

Chapter 14

Strategies for Success and Expansion

Once a small business has established itself, it may look to expand and grow further. The following are some strategies for success and expansion:

1. **Diversification:** Diversifying your product or service offerings can help your business grow and mitigate risk. This can include expanding into new markets, developing new products or services, or entering into new partnerships.

2. **Innovation:** Continuously innovating and improving your products and services can help your business stay ahead of the competition and meet the evolving needs of your customers. Investing in research and development, as well as staying up-to-date with industry trends, can help you bring innovative products and services to market.

3. **Customer Satisfaction:** Focusing on customer satisfaction and providing exceptional customer service can help your business build a loyal customer base and attract new customers through word-of-mouth. Regularly gathering customer feedback and making improvements based on their suggestions can help you stay ahead of the competition.

4. **Efficient Operations:** Streamlining operations and increasing efficiency can help your business increase profitability and better meet the needs of your customers. This can include

implementing new technologies, automating processes, and reducing waste.

5. **Strategic Partnerships:** Developing strategic partnerships and collaborations with other businesses, suppliers, and industry organizations can help you expand your reach, access new resources, and stay ahead of the competition.

6. **Employee Development:** Investing in the development and training of your employees can help your business attract and retain top talent and improve overall performance. Providing opportunities for employees to grow and advance within your organization can also help build a strong company culture and drive success.

7. **Financial Management:** Effective financial management is crucial for the success and expansion of your business. This includes monitoring cash flow, keeping accurate records, and making informed investment decisions. Working with a financial advisor or accountant can help you make informed financial decisions and ensure the long-term success of your business.

8. **Networking:** Building a solid network of contacts within your industry can help you stay informed of industry trends, connect with potential customers and partners, and find new opportunities for growth. Participating in industry events, joining professional organizations, and reaching out to mentors can help you build and expand your network.

9. **Online Presence:** Establishing a strong online presence can help your business reach a wider audience and increase visibility. This can include creating a website, building a

social media presence, and leveraging digital marketing strategies such as search engine optimization (SEO) and pay-per-click advertising (PPC).

10. **Continuous Learning:** Staying informed of industry trends and best practices can help your business stay ahead of the competition and continuously improve. Attending workshops, conferences, and webinars, as well as reading industry publications, can help you stay informed and learn from experts in your field.
11. **Adaptability:** Being able to quickly adapt to changes in the market and industry can help your business stay relevant and competitive. This can include embracing new technologies, adjusting product or service offerings, and pivoting your business strategy as needed.

Success and expansion for a small business require a combination of hard work, determination, and strategic planning. By continuously innovating, building a strong brand, and focusing on customer satisfaction, small businesses can achieve sustained growth and success.

Chapter 15

Conclusion and Next Steps for Your Small Business Venture

Starting and growing a small business can be a challenging but rewarding journey. In this book, we have explored various small business ideas, as well as the steps involved in launching and operating a successful business venture.

In the final chapter of this book, it's important to reflect on what you have learned and plan for the next steps.

1. **Recap:** Take some time to review the key points and strategies discussed in the book and reflect on what you have learned.
2. **Assess your progress:** Evaluate where you are in your business journey and what still needs to be done. This can include conducting market research, securing funding, building your brand, and establishing your online presence.
3. **Set goals:** Based on your assessment, set achievable and measurable goals for the short and long term. This can include sales targets, customer acquisition goals, and milestones for expanding your business.
4. **Create an action plan:** Develop a plan of action to achieve your goals, including specific steps, deadlines, and milestones.
5. **Seek advice and support:** Don't be afraid to seek advice and support from mentors, business advisors, and professional organizations. This can include finding a business coach,

joining a business incubator, or participating in entrepreneurship programs.
6. **Stay focused and committed:** Running a small business can be challenging, but with hard work, dedication, and perseverance, you can achieve success. Stay focused on your goals and keep pushing forward, even when faced with obstacles and setbacks.
7. **Continuously evaluate and adapt:** The business environment is constantly evolving, and it's important to stay up-to-date with industry trends and changes. Regularly evaluate your business, and be open to making changes and adjustments as needed.
8. **Celebrate your successes:** Don't forget to celebrate your accomplishments and milestones along the way. This can help to maintain your motivation and keep you focused on your goals.
9. **Network and connect:** Building relationships and connecting with other small business owners and entrepreneurs can be valuable in terms of sharing experiences, learning from others, and finding new opportunities. Attend industry events, join business organizations, and participate in online communities to expand your network.
10. **Give back:** As your small business grows and succeeds, consider giving back to your community and supporting causes that are important to you. This can include volunteering, making donations, or participating in local events.

Starting a small business is not only about achieving success but also about making a positive impact on others and contributing to your community. By following the steps outlined in this book, you can launch and grow a successful small business that realizes your dreams and aspirations while making a difference in the world.

www.ingramcontent.com/pod-product-compliance
Lightning Source LLC
Chambersburg PA
CBHW050241220526
45465CB00017B/824